Tracing Sight Words Worksheets
Tracing Sight Words For Kindergarten

to

I came to help!

to   to   to   to

Find and trace the word **to**

to   to   see
my   to   THE   is
    for   to

to

Draw a picture of the sentence

Go to school.

Go to

to

Table of Contents – 100 Sight Words

a	40	for	9	just	70	put	55	use	107
about	106	from	58	know	72	said	19	want	48
again	74	funny	76	like	44	saw	34	was	25
all	47	get	88	little	37	see	12	we	7
and	17	go	15	look	21	she	33	were	65
are	22	going	66	made	86	so	42	what	28
as	90	good	54	make	94	some	77	when	64
at	81	had	89	me	20	soon	57	where	14
away	51	has	68	my	8	take	78	who	31
be	52	have	26	new	50	than	99	would	102
been	112	he	32	no	53	that	84	you	10
but	97	her	56	not	103	the	6	your	83
by	61	here	29	now	46	their	109	REVIEW	16
came	45	him	108	of	59	them	79	REVIEW	27
can	114	his	69	on	96	then	67	REVIEW	38
come	18	how	92	once	75	there	36	REVIEW	49
could	62	I	23	or	85	these	111	REVIEW	60
did	91	if	87	other	101	they	35	REVIEW	71
do	24	in	113	our	43	this	98	REVIEW	82
each	100	is	11	out	110	to	13	REVIEW	93
every	63	it	95	play	39	too	41	REVIEW	104
find	30	its	105	please	80	under	73	REVIEW	115

Instructions For Use

Tracing Worksheets

1. Read the sight word and sentence
2. Copy the sight word
3. Find and trace the sight word
4. Trace the sight word then write it on your own
5. Trace the sentence
6. Trace and fill in the rest of the sentence
7. Draw a picture to match the sentence

Tic-Tac-Toe Review

1. Each player picks a sight word and writes it on their line
2. Take turns writing your sight word in a spot on the tic-tac-toe
3. First to three in a row wins

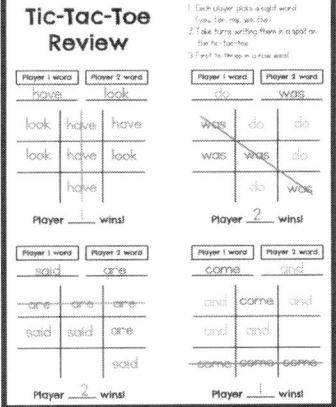

Roll and Write

1. Pick 6 sight words, write one on each line on the bottom row above the dice
2. Roll a dice and find the number on your paper
3. Write the sight word in the column
4. Whichever sight word reaches the top first wins

REVIEW: Word Search

1. Pick a word from the word bank
2. Find it in the word search
3. Trace it
4. Cross off the word in the word bank
5. Find them all

the

I am the best!

the the the the

Find and trace the word **the**

the   *of*   the

you   say   you

the   me   the

the

Draw a picture of the sentence

The boy fell.

The boy

The

we

We always try.

we   we   we   we

Find and trace the word we

the   for   say

we   we   you

        we

can   we

we

Draw a picture of the sentence

We will eat it.

We will

We

I'm grateful for my mind.

my my my my

Find and trace the word my

can   my   do

we   we   for   my

my   my

my

Draw a picture of the sentence

My bug jumps.

My bug

My

for

I will look for good in all.

---

for for for for

Find and trace the word for

can   say   am

for   For   do

     for

yes   for

---

for

Draw a picture of the sentence	Go for it!
	Go for
	for

you

You are amazing!

you you you you

Find and trace the word YOU

you   you   am

for   do   yes   you

you   is

you

Draw a picture of the sentence

I see you.

see you.

you.

is

It is good to be here.

is   is   is   is

Find and trace the word is

is   the   my

is   is   IS   we

you   for

is

Draw a picture of the sentence

She is happy.

She is

She

see

I see the good in me.

---

see see see see

Find and trace the word see

we   you   see

see   see

the   my   is   **see**

---

see

Draw a picture of the sentence

See it smells!

See it

See

I came to help!

to to to to

Find and trace the word to

to
to
see

my
the
is

to

for
to

to

Draw a picture of the sentence

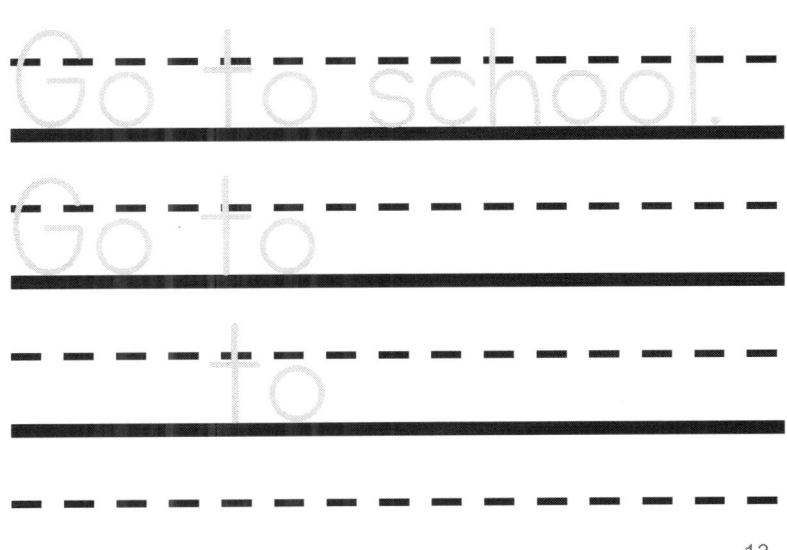

Go to school.

Go to

to

where

**I see where
I can help.**

where where where

Find and trace the word where

you   to   see

for   **where**   WHERE   **is**

where   where

where

Draw a picture of the sentence

Where is it?

Where is

Where

go

Go get them!

go   go   go   go

Find and trace the word go

go   you   go

where   is   TO   go

go   see

go

Draw a picture of the sentence

I will go too.

I   go

go

Roll and Write

1. Pick 6 sight words, write one on each line on the bottom row above the dice
2. Roll a dice and find the number on your paper
3. Write the sight word in the column
4. Whichever sight word reaches the top first wins!

winner!	winner!	winner!	winner!	winner!	winner!
_____	_____	_____	_____	_____	_____

and

I can be
happy and sad.

---

and   and   and

Find and trace the word and

to   my   you

and   and   **and**

        see

and   go

and

Draw a picture of the sentence

Sand and sea.

Sand and

and

come

Come and play
with us!

come come come

Find and trace the word come

come   to   come

go   we   the

where   come   come

come

Draw a picture of the sentence

Come see it!

Come see

Come

said

I said you're welcome!

said said said

Find and trace the word **said**

to said go

for **said** SAID come

said is

said

Draw a picture of the sentence

I said hello.

I said

said

me

Can you help me?

me me me me

Find and trace the word me

we
me
me
my
me
said
for
me
where

me

Draw a picture of the sentence

You saved me!

You saved

You

look

I will look
for the good.

look   look   look

Find and trace the word **look**

look   *look*   for

look   **said**   LOOK   is

and   come

look

Draw a picture of the sentence

You look nice!

You look

look

are

You are the best!

are   are   are   are

Find and trace the word are

the   are   are

are   say   you

are   me   for

are

Draw a picture of the sentence

Are you sad?

Are you

Are

I

I like to play.

I I I I

Find and trace the word I

I we my

you I

say I l

I the

I

Draw a picture of the sentence

I am happy.
I am
am

do

I will do my best!

do   do   do   do

Find and trace the word do

I my	do		do
	the	you	**do**
do		the	

do

<table>
<tr><td>Draw a picture of the sentence</td><td>I do chores.</td></tr>
<tr><td></td><td>I do</td></tr>
<tr><td></td><td>do</td></tr>
</table>

was

The cat was happy.

was   was   was

was   do   was

me   the   was   you

was   look

was

Draw a picture of the sentence

He was sad.

He was

was

have

We will have fun!

have   have   have

have   have   have

look   are   THE   **have**

me   the

have

Draw a picture of the sentence

I have a dog.

I have a

have

Tic-Tac-Toe Review

1. Each player picks a sight word and writes it on their line
2. Take turns writing your sight word in a spot on the tic-tac-toe
3. First to three in a row wins

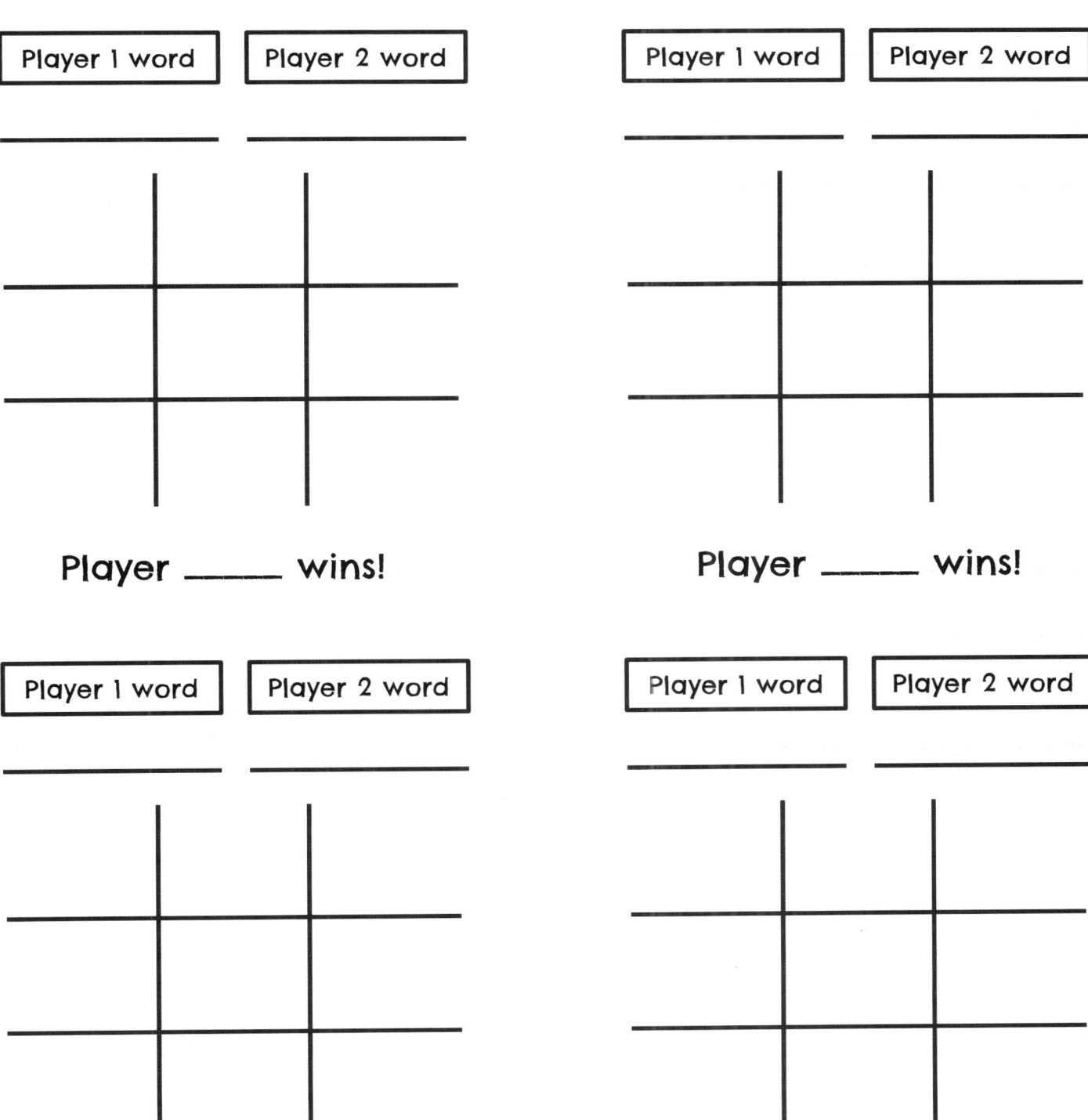

Player 1 word | Player 2 word

Player _____ wins!

Player 1 word | Player 2 word

Player _____ wins!

Player 1 word | Player 2 word

Player _____ wins!

Player 1 word | Player 2 word

Player _____ wins!

What is that?

what what what

Find and trace the word **what**

do
was
are

what
what
Have

what
the

what

What is that?

What is

What

here

I like it here.

here here here

Find and trace the word here

look here do

you say here

here me say here

here

Draw a picture of the sentence

I am here.

I am here.

here

find

I will find the lost toy.

find   find   find

Find and trace the word find

find   said   find

find   DO   you

me   **find**   the

find

Draw a picture of the sentence

Find the cat.
Find the
Find

Who are you?

who   who   who

Find and trace the word who

here   *who*   I

the   **find**   say   you

who   who

who

Draw a picture of the sentence

Who are you?

Who are

Who

he

He is my friend!

he he he he

Find and trace the word he

he
find   you   he
          he   say
me   he   who

he

Draw a picture of the sentence

He is big!

He is

He

she

She is kind.

she she she she

Find and trace the word **she**

here she the

who she so

she he

she

Draw a picture of the sentence

She is kind.

She is

She

saw

You saw the icecream truck!

saw   saw   saw

Find and trace the word saw

she   saw   saw

saw   DO   are

was   saw   here

saw

Draw a picture of the sentence

I saw a hog.

I saw

saw

They are grateful for you!

they   they   they

Find and trace the word **they**

they   who   they

do   was   what

they   **they**

they   come

they

Draw a picture of the sentence

They can run.

They can

They

there

There is good
in each day.

there there there

Find and trace the word **there**

for   *there*   find

there   WHO   **there**

here   **go**   *there*

there

Draw a picture of the sentence

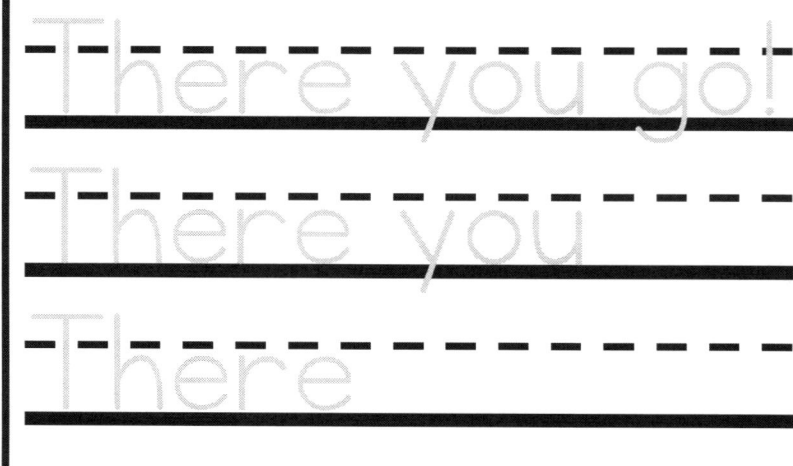

There you go!

There you

There

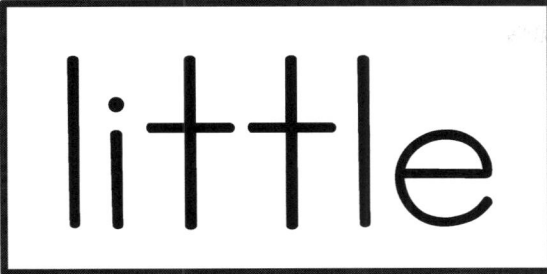

I am a little bit scared!

little little little

Find and trace the word **little**

saw   little   my

was   **little**   LITTLE   see

who   little

little

Draw a picture of the sentence

A little mouse.

A little

little

Roll and
Write

1. Pick 6 sight words, write one on each line on the bottom row above the dice
2. Roll a dice and find the number on your paper
3. Write the sight word in the column
4. Whichever sight word reaches the top first wins!

winner!	winner!	winner!	winner!	winner!	winner!
_ _ _ _	_ _ _ _	_ _ _ _	_ _ _ _	_ _ _ _	_ _ _ _

play

I will play with you!

play   play   play

look   you   play

play   play   said   play

the   there

play

Draw a picture of the sentence

I play outside.

I play

play

a

He is a cool friend.

a a a a

find a little

play have a the

a a

a

Draw a picture of the sentence

A cat naps.

A cat

A

too

I will go too!

too too too too

little   there   too

too   me   too

too

have   look

too

Draw a picture of the sentence

I ate it too.

I ate too.

too.

SO

There is so much to see!

so   so   so   so

Find and trace the word SO

so   here   so

what   so   so   she

was   he

so

Draw a picture of the sentence

I am so tired.

I am so

I   so

our

Our friends will
be so glad.

our our our our

our   I   our

do   come   look

our   little

our

Draw a picture of the sentence

See our bird?

See our

our

like

I like to draw pictures.

like like like like

Find and trace the word like

you   like   my

is   like   LIKE   we

she   like

like

Draw a picture of the sentence

I like my cup.

I like my

like

came

We came in first.

came came came

Find and trace the word came

see *the* **came**

to **came** she

came *came*

came

Draw a picture of the sentence

I came home.

I came

came

now

Now we can do it too.

now   now   now

Find and trace the word now

have   *now*   **now**

who   GO   **now**

what   **now**

                          where

now

Draw a picture of the sentence

Now I get it!

Now I

Now

all

I am keeping it all!

all all all all

Find and trace the word all

are all all
all was find
have here
all

all

Draw a picture of the sentence

You see it all.
You it all.
all.

want

I want to hang out with you.

want want want

Find and trace the word want

come   want   look

said   me   want   I

want   want

want

Draw a picture of the sentence

Want to sing?

Want to

Want

Tic-Tac-Toe Review

1. Each player picks a sight word and writes it on their line
2. Take turns writing your sight word in a spot on the tic-tac-toe
3. First to three in a row wins

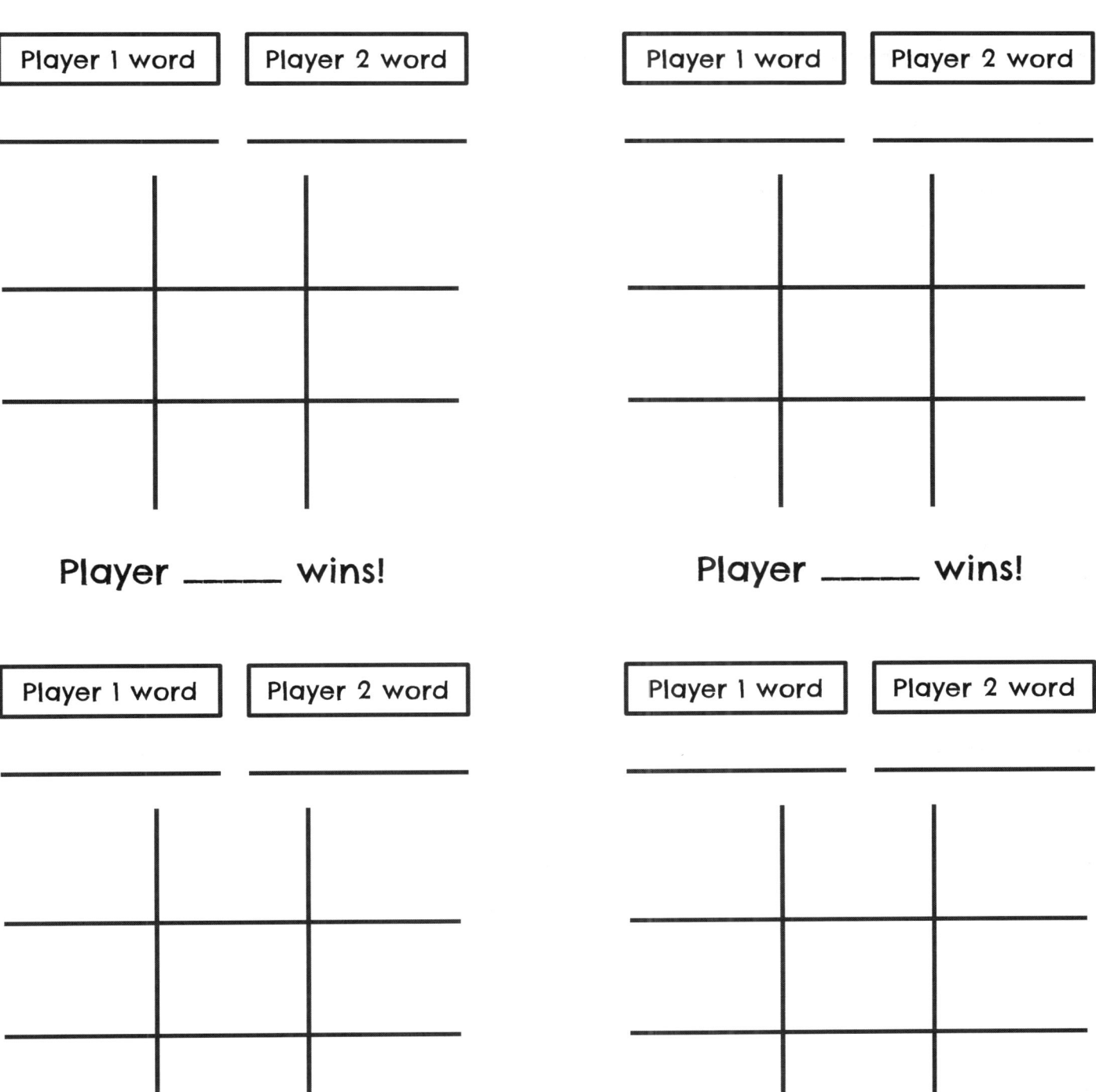

| Player 1 word | Player 2 word |

Player _____ wins!

| Player 1 word | Player 2 word |

Player _____ wins!

| Player 1 word | Player 2 word |

Player _____ wins!

| Player 1 word | Player 2 word |

Player _____ wins!

new

I have new shoes.

new new new

Find and trace the word new

to   go   where

new   new   new   new

see   and

new

Draw a picture of the sentence

The new lock.

The new

new

I miss you when you are away.

away away away

Find and trace the word **away**

away so

away

was my He look

away

away

away

Draw a picture of the sentence

It blew away.

It away.

away.

be

Let's be friends forever!

be   be   be   be

Find and trace the word be

me   be   be

be   said   Be   and

look   come

be

Draw a picture of the sentence

Be brave, go!

Be brave,

Be

no

No, I don't have gum.

no   no   no   no

Find and trace the word no

no   do   are

have   I   no

no   no

was

no

Draw a picture of the sentence

No, that's mine.

No, that's

No

good

We are good to go!

good good good

Find and trace the word good

good good find
what GOOD who
here
good he
good

good

Draw a picture of the sentence

Good job kid!

Good job

Good

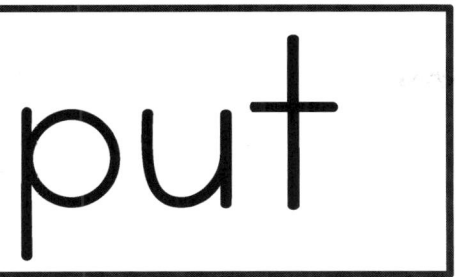

You can put that here.

put put put put

Find and trace the word put

and *put* she

put come he

for **put** *put*

put

Draw a picture of the sentence

Put it back.

Put it

Put

her

Her notebook is cool.

her her her her

put   came   her

her   LIKe   **her**

do

her   now

her

Draw a picture of the sentence

Go ask her.

Go ____ her.

____ her

soon

My birthday is so soon!

soon   soon   soon

Find and trace the word soon

play   soon   there

soon   soon   saw

        soon   she

little

soon

Draw a picture of the sentence

It is soon!

It   soon!

soon

from

Where are you from?

from from from

Find and trace the word **from**

from who from

what FIND he

from

here from

from

Draw a picture of the sentence

It's from me!

It's from

from

of

I'm full of candy.

- - - of - of - of - of - of - - -

here and me
of come of
of said
of

- - - of - - - - - - - - - - - - -

Draw a picture of the sentence

Birds of prey.

Birds of

of

REVIEW: Word Search

Copy each word in the word search then cross it off in the word bank

Word Bank:				
the	is	and	saw	too
my	see	said	they	so
for	where	me	little	our
you	go	look	play	like

```
w  g  d  f  l  i  t  t  l  e
h  t  h  e  t  e  v  w  m  p
e  p  l  a  y  u  s  e  e  o
r  c  s  i  t  o  o  x  y  q
e  h  r  s  a  w  l  o  o  k
i  s  o  q  n  t  h  e  y  r
j  f  o  r  l  m  s  a  i  d
b  k  l  i  k  e  v  u  o  s
g  o  w  z  a  n  d  t  u  z
m  y  a  x  y  y  w  x  r  z
```

I'll come by your class.

by   by   by   by

Find and trace the word **by**

and   by   came

said   For   **what**

by   **put**   by

by

Draw a picture of the sentence

Stand by me.

Stand by

by

could

We could get a dog?

could   could   could

Find and trace the word could

could   soon   like

we   COULD   have

         are

     could   I

could

Draw a picture of the sentence

Could we ask?

Could we

Could

every

I counted every car.

every every every

play   soon   every

every   GO   soon

little   every

every

every

Draw a picture of the sentence

Every red can.

Every red

Every

when

When will you eat?

when when when

when   when   come

and   said   when

when   look   me

when

Draw a picture of the sentence

I'll say when.

I'll   when.

when

were

They were running fast.

were were were

Find and trace the word were

now   were   all
were   were   want
        were
    came   new

were

Draw a picture of the sentence	

going

We are going to draw.

going going going

the going going

we GOING what

going then by

going

Draw a picture of the sentence

I'm going too.

I'm going

going

then

First we swim,
then we eat!

then then then

Find and trace the word **then**

then my we

for THEN the

then

you then

then

Draw a picture of the sentence

Spin then run.

Spin then

then

has

She has been
happy you came!

has has has has

Find and trace the word has

has   has   to

go   where   see

        has

has   is

has

Draw a picture of the sentence

He has blue.

He has

has

his

His ice cream
is melting.

his   his   his   his

Find and trace the word his

come   said   me

and   HIS   his

his   look

his

Draw a picture of the sentence

His team won.

His team

His

I just want to play!

just just just just

Find and trace the word just

just	do	just
are	I	have
just	was	just

just

Draw a picture of the sentence

Just get up!

Just get

Just

Roll and Write

1. Pick 6 sight words, write one on each line on the bottom row above the dice
2. Roll a dice and find the number on your paper
3. Write the sight word in the column
4. Whichever sight word reaches the top first wins!

winner!	winner!	winner!	winner!	winner!	winner!
_____	_____	_____	_____	_____	_____

I know how
to do that.

know know know

Find and trace the word know

have   *like*   know

know   **know**   GO   **now**

what   know

know

Draw a picture of the sentence

I know you!

I know

know

under

I walk under
the bridge.

under under under

under   under   where

who   know   now

what   **under**   under

under

Draw a picture of the sentence

Look under it.

Look under

under

again

He can play that again.

again again again

again   We   again

who   again   now

again   I   where

again

Draw a picture of the sentence

Do it again!

Do it again!

again

once

Once upon a time.

once once once

Find and trace the word once

have
once
once
once

now

GO

once
we
where

once

Draw a picture of the sentence

Say it once.

Say once.

once

funny

That was funny!

funny funny funny

Find and trace the word funny

have　　　now　　　funny

funny　　　　　　　FUNNY　　the

what　　find

funny

funny

Draw a picture of the sentence	He is funny!
	He funny!
	funny!

some

Some people like snow.

some some some

some   me   have

here   some   some

was

some   the

some

Draw a picture of the sentence

Some kids nap.

Some kids

Some

take

He will take it.

take take take

Find and trace the word take

take ~~of~~ the

you take

are **take** me take

take

Draw a picture of the sentence

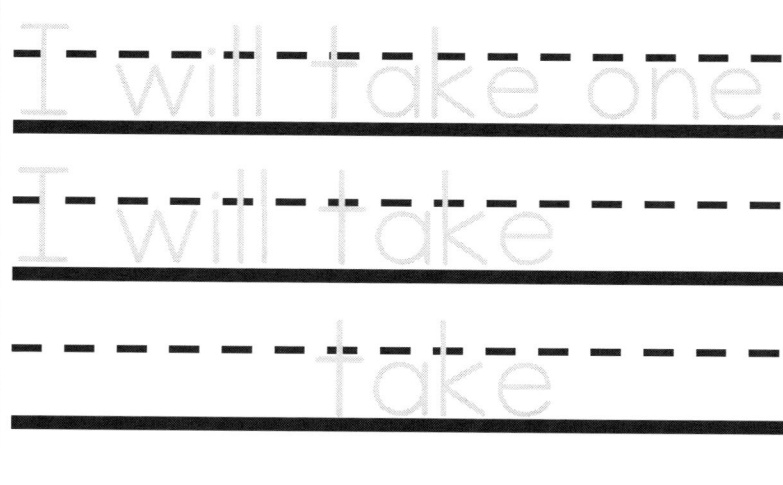

I will take one.

I will take

take

them

Be kind to them.

them them them

Find and trace the word **them**

them
them
here
say
of
are
she
you
them

them

Draw a picture of the sentence

I have them.
I ___ them.
___ them

please

Help me please!

please please please

Find and trace the word please

take please please

you say them

me please please

please

Draw a picture of the sentence

Help please!

please!

please

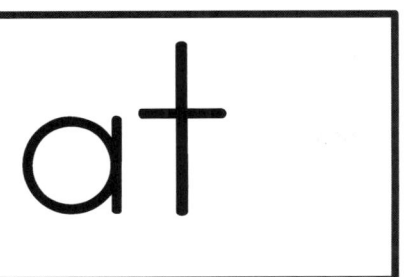

She is good at that.

at   at   at   at

Find and trace the word at

please   of   at

at   at   at   **me**

are   some

at

Draw a picture of the sentence

Tic-Tac-Toe Review

1. Each player picks a sight word and writes it on their line
2. Take turns writing your sight word in a spot on the tic-tac-toe
3. First to three in a row wins

Player 1 word	Player 2 word

Player _____ wins!

Player 1 word	Player 2 word

Player _____ wins!

Player 1 word	Player 2 word

Player _____ wins!

Player 1 word	Player 2 word

Player _____ wins!

your

Is that your work?

your your your

Find and trace the word **your**

who   your   your

fine   Here   **your**

your

he   what

your

Draw a picture of the sentence

Your little cat.

Your little

Your

That would be so helpful.

that that that

Find and trace the word **that**

she   *that*   they

that   saw   **there**

that   **that**   little

that

Draw a picture of the sentence

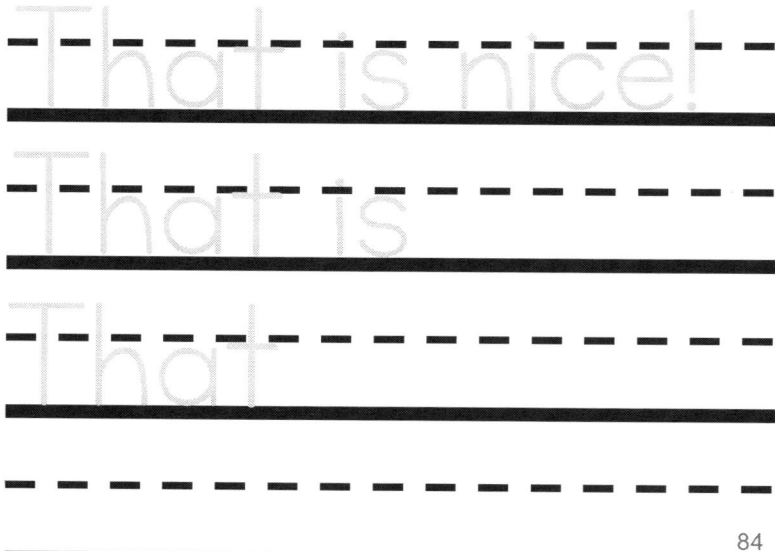

That is nice!

That is

That

or

Chocolate or vanilla?

or   or   or   or

Find and trace the word or

a   or   or

too   or   play

        our

    so   or

or

Draw a picture of the sentence

Day or night?

Day or

or

made

I made this just for you.

made made made

Find and trace the word made

made   made   now

like   came   all

made   **made**

made   want

made

Draw a picture of the sentence

You made it!

You made

made

If you are sad
I can help.

if if if if

Find and trace the word if

if   be   no
new   IF   if
if   away   good

if

Draw a picture of the sentence

If it rains.

If it

If

get

I get to sit by you!

get get get get

Find and trace the word get

put   get   get

get   soon   from

        her

get   of

get

Draw a picture of the sentence

I get it.

I get

I get

had

I wish we had all day.

had had had had

Find and trace the word **had**

when   had   by

were   COULD   **had**

every   **had**   had

had

Draw a picture of the sentence

We had it.

We had

had

as

You are as bright
as the sun!

as   as   as   as

Find and trace the word as

going   as   as

then   Has   his

        as

as   just

as

Draw a picture of the sentence

Dark as night.

Dark as

as

did

You did it!

did did did did

Find and trace the word **did**

again   under   did

once   DID   know

funny   did   did

did

Draw a picture of the sentence

Did you do it?

Did you

Did

How are you feeling?

how how how

Find and trace the word how

how please take

how HOW how

at them some

how

Draw a picture of the sentence

How is it?

How is

How

Roll and Write

1. Pick 6 sight words, write one on each line on the bottom row above the dice
2. Roll a dice and find the number on your paper
3. Write the sight word in the column
4. Whichever sight word reaches the top first wins!

winner!	winner!	winner!	winner!	winner!	winner!
_____	_____	_____	_____	_____	_____

make

Make me some cookies please!

make make make

Find and trace the word make

them   make   some

please   take   at

make   **make**   make

make

Draw a picture of the sentence

Make my bed.

Make my

Make

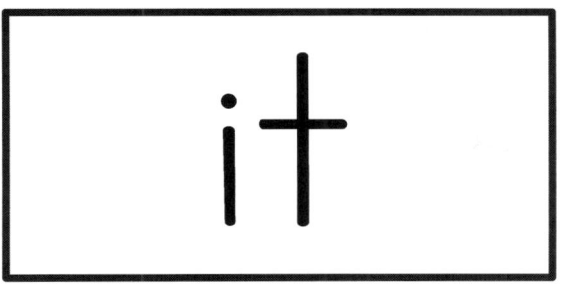

It would be amazing!

it it it it

Find and trace the word it

your   or   it

that   IT   it

it   made   if

it

Draw a picture of the sentence

It is so good.

It is

It

on

You are on an awesome journey!

on   on   on   on

Find and trace the word on

did   on   has

every   on   get

on

how   on

on

Draw a picture of the sentence

You are on it.

You   on

on

but

But can you go with me?

but but but but

but   but   the
but   you   we
but   for   my

but

Draw a picture of the sentence

But it's loud!

But it's

But

this

This game went fast.

this this this this

this   too   this

is   THIS   where

this   see   go

this

Draw a picture of the sentence

This is fun!

This is fun

This

I'm sleepier than a baby.

than than than

Find and trace the word **than**

said   look   and

than   come   **than**

than

me   than

than

Draw a picture of the sentence

Bluer than me.

Bluer than

than

each

We each get half.

each   each   each

Find and trace the word each

each   I   each

are   was   each

do

each   have

each

Draw a picture of the sentence

Each lid fits.

Each lid

Each

other

All the other kids are glad to see you.

other other other

Find and trace the word other

other other every

every OTHER soon

other

little every

other

Draw a picture of the sentence

Every other.

other.

other

Would you like to join us?

would would would

Find and trace the word would

have   would   I

was   are

    would   do

would   would

would

Draw a picture of the sentence

Yes it would.

Yes would.

would

They did not get dirty.

not not not not

Find and trace the word not

not   here   find

what   not   who

not   he

not

Draw a picture of the sentence

Not in here.

Not in

Not

Tic-Tac-Toe Review

1. Each player picks a sight word and writes it on their line
2. Take turns writing your sight word in a spot on the tic-tac-toe
3. First to three in a row wins

Player 1 word	Player 2 word

Player _____ wins!

Player 1 word	Player 2 word

Player _____ wins!

Player 1 word	Player 2 word

Player _____ wins!

Player 1 word	Player 2 word

Player _____ wins!

its

Its owner is the girl in blue.

its its its its

Find and trace the word **its**

saw   *its*   there

its   THEY   **look**

she   **its**   its

its

Draw a picture of the sentence

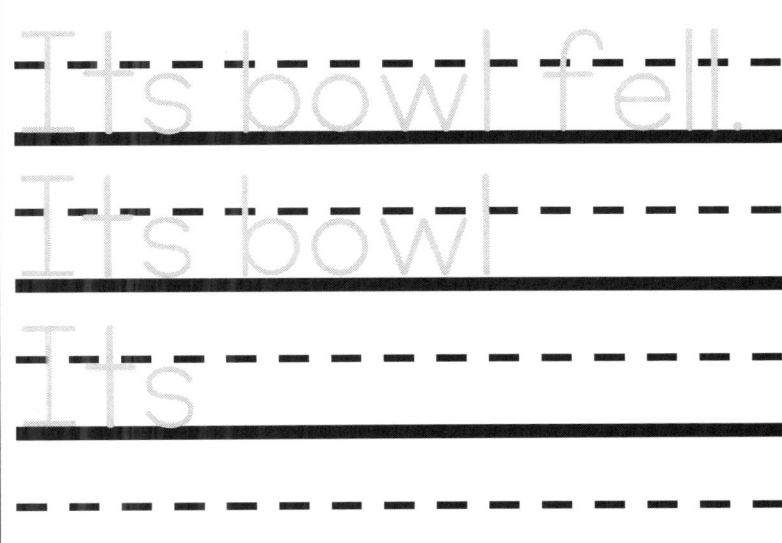

Its bowl fell.

Its bowl

Its

about

I love to learn about science.

about about about

Find and trace the word about

could play so

about ABOUT our

about a too

about

Draw a picture of the sentence

It's about me.

It's about

about

use

I use all the crayons.

use use use use

Find and trace the word use

bye   use   use

could   use   like

      use

little   came

use

Draw a picture of the sentence

Use red there.

Use red

Use

That gift is for him.

him him him him

Find and trace the word him

him him know

funny under him

again

once him

him

Draw a picture of the sentence

That is him.

That is

That

It was their turn.

their their their

Find and trace the word **their**

get had their
their as did
their their how

their

Draw a picture of the sentence

See their map.
See their
their

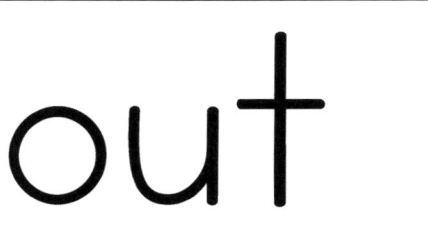

I'll go out
there with you.

out out out out

Find and trace the word **OUT**

out   by   out

said   OUT   **what**

   by   **put**   out

out

Draw a picture of the sentence

Spit it out.

Spit out.

out.

these

These are so
fun to do!

these these these

Find and trace the word **these**

make   these   this

it   THESE   but

these   on   these

these

Draw a picture of the sentence

These go up.

These go

These

been

It's been so long since I've seen you.

been been been

Find and trace the word **been**

had   been   had

get   HOW   **been**

        been

been   did

been

Draw a picture of the sentence

It's been fun.

It's been

been

in

Will you stay in with me?

in   in   in   in

Find and trace the word in

in   other   in

would   each   **than**

in   not   in

in

Draw a picture of the sentence

In the cubby.

In the

In

can

Can you hear me?

can can can can

Find and trace the word can

going   then   has

can   can   can

    just   his

can

can

Draw a picture of the sentence

Can I go ?

Can I

Can

REVIEW: Word Search

Copy each word in the word search then cross it off in the word bank

<table>
<tr><td rowspan="4">Word Bank:</td><td>could</td><td>then</td><td>again</td><td>your</td><td>each</td></tr>
<tr><td>every</td><td>just</td><td>once</td><td>made</td><td>get</td></tr>
<tr><td>when</td><td>know</td><td>funny</td><td>how</td><td>about</td></tr>
<tr><td>going</td><td>under</td><td>some</td><td>make</td><td>been</td></tr>
</table>

```
z  f  e  v  e  r  y  u  a  t
c  u  h  o  w  q  o  n  b  h
o  n  y  b  h  u  u  d  o  e
u  n  v  e  e  v  r  e  u  n
l  y  w  e  n  j  w  r  t  x
d  x  m  n  r  u  m  a  k  e
a  g  a  i  n  s  o  n  c  e
u  e  d  r  p  t  s  o  m  e
t  t  e  s  q  k  n  o  w  y
g  o  i  n  g  e  a  c  h  z
```

Terms Of Use

This product is the intellectual property of Resource Teacher's Guide all rights reserved, and may only be used for personal classroom use by one single teacher. This product may not be copied, modified, repackaged, resold, shared or distributed; this includes making copies for other teachers. You may purchase an additional license for a discounted price by going to "my purchases" and clicking "buy additional licenses". You may not copy any part of this product to place on personal websites, blogs, classroom websites, or district websites.

www.resourceteachersguide.com

Made in the USA
Columbia, SC
22 February 2025